# The Jesup North Pacific Expedition

Edited by FRANZ BOAS

## VOL. 2

### PART II

AMS PRESS
NEW YORK

# The Jesup North Pacific Expedition

Edited by Franz Boas

---

## Memoir of the American Museum

of

## Natural History

NEW YORK

---

VOL. II — PART II

CAIRNS OF BRITISH COLUMBIA

AND WASHINGTON

BY

HARLAN INGERSOLL SMITH

AND  GERARD FOWKE

NEW YORK, 1901

Library of Congress Cataloging in Publication Data

Smith, Harlan Ingersoll, 1872-1940.
  Cairns of British Columbia and Washington.

    Reprint of the 1901 ed. published in New York, which was issued as v. 4
of Memoirs of the American Museum of Natural History, Anthropology, v. 3,
pt. 2, and as v. 2, pt. 2 of Publications of the Jesup North Pacific Expedition.
    1. Indians of North America—British Columbia—Antiquities.  2. Indians of
North America—Washington (State)—Antiquities.  3. British Columbia—
Antiquities.  4. Washington (State)— Antiquities.  I. Fowke, Gerard, 1855-
1933, joint author.  II. Title.  III. Series: American Museum of Natural
History, New York. Memoirs ; v. 4.  IV. Series: The Jesup North Pacific
Expedition. Publications ; v. 2, pt. 2.
E78.B9S64  1975                    971.1                    73-3517
ISBN 0-404-58118-8

Reprinted from the edition of 1901, New York
First AMS edition published, 1975
Manufactured in the United States of America

International Standard Book Number:
Complete Set:    0-404-58100-5
Volume 2 pt. 2:  0-404-58118-8

AMS PRESS, INC.
New York, N.Y. 10003

# LIST OF ILLUSTRATIONS.

*TEXT FIGURES.*

Cairns of British Columbia and Washington.

# II.—Cairns of British Columbia and Washington.

By Harlan I. Smith and Gerard Fowke.

## GENERAL DESCRIPTION.

In the southeastern part of Vancouver Island in British Columbia, and on the San Juan Group and Whidbey Island in Washington, numerous stone cairns containing graves are found. All of these, so far as known, are of considerable age. They certainly antedate the period of the first advent of objects manufactured by whites. The Indians have no historic tradition as to their origin.

The cairns (Plate I) are from three to twenty feet in diameter, and generally consist of irregular piles of bowlders. In some cases a more or less rectangular cyst is built around the body (Plate II), made by roughly placing together a number of bowlders, the straightest sides of which are placed so as to form an oblong cyst, and by covering the opening thus formed with one, two, or more slab-shaped rocks, each extending from side to side. These we will call "cover-stones." No cairns were found where two or more stones were wedged over the cyst in the manner of an arch. In other cases there are slab-like stones over the grave, but the cyst is ill defined, if present at all. In still other cases the enclosure is well made, but the stones used to cover the top are so small that they do not reach across. Above the cyst a rough pile of stones is reared. Many cairns are bounded by single rows of large stones, while the space between this outer wall and the cyst is filled with small fragments of bowlders, and in some cases largely with soil or with a mixture of these materials (Plates I, Fig. 1 ; III, Fig. 2). Several cairns have been found where the outer row of stones had been laid in a rectangle and carried up so as to form a retaining-wall, making the whole structure resemble a truncated pyramid (Plate IV, Fig. 1). Other cairns have been found in which the body rested at the side of a large bowlder, and was covered with small bowlders piled up against the large rock (Plates I, Fig. 2 ; V, Fig. 2). The stones forming the cyst and those in the outer row are often embedded deep in the soil around the grave. Probably they were not so placed, but sank to this position by reason of their large size and great weight. In some cases the stones of the cyst project above the rest of the cairn (Plate V, Fig. 2).

The position of the skeletons proves that the bodies were placed on the side, with the usual flexion (Plate III, Fig. 1). They were deposited either on the original surface of the soil, or in a shallow hole dug down into the surface soil or even into the gravel below. In some cases the skeletons are found sunk into the soil. Many of them are much decayed. This is especially the case in the cairns near Victoria, B. C., in which complete skulls are rarely obtained.   In forty-two cairns opened there, no entire bones were secured.   At North Saanich, B. C., and near Coupeville, Wash., however, complete skeletons have been collected. A few of these were partly burned, but the burning probably did not take place in the cairns.

A few copper ornaments have been found buried with the skeletons, and in one cairn a stone object was secured from among the top stones (Figs. 2 and 4, pp. 65, 68).   Bancroft[1] states that in a rectangular cairn near Comox, B. C., a pencil-shaped stone, sharp at both ends, was found with a skeleton.   Objects other than these have not been found, except in cairns built on shell-heaps, as at North Saanich.   But objects found in these cairns do not seem to be in positions suggesting that they were buried with the bodies, and their presence may be satisfactorily accounted for by assuming that they were taken up from the shell-heaps with the earth or bowlders used in the construction of the cairn.

The scarcity in these cairns of all objects other than human bones is remarkable.   In this respect the cairns resemble the graves in the shell-heaps of Lower Fraser River, where, excepting a few pieces of copper, hardly any specimens were found associated with skeletons, notwithstanding the wealth of material obtained from the shell-layers near by.

The cairns on Vancouver Island near Victoria and Comox have been known for many years, and are described by Bancroft,[2] from information furnished by Mr. James Deans of Victoria, and embodying the results of examinations made by him in 1871.   Mr. James Richardson, of the Canadian Geological Survey, was one of the first to open cairns.   Those near Victoria, being convenient of access, have since been examined by numerous investigators, including Professor Karl von den Steinen and members of the Natural History Society of Victoria.   Prominent among the latter were Dr. Charles F. Newcombe and Mr. O. C. Hastings. Some osteological material resulting from their work is preserved in the Provincial Museum in Victoria.   Professor Franz Boas examined a number of cairns at Parsons Bridge, near Victoria, and on the Saanich Peninsula.   Dr. George A. Dorsey excavated a few at Cadboro Bay in 1897.

The following description is based on explorations conducted for the Jesup North Pacific Expedition in the years 1897, 1898, and 1899.   A detailed statement of these is given on pp. 60 *et seq*.   With the exception of the explorations made by Mr. Fowke in 1898, the whole work was carried on under the direction of Mr. Smith.

In our investigations near Cadboro Bay, assistance was rendered by Mr. O. C. Hastings and Mr. James Deans ; at Comox and North Saanich, by Mr. Albert A. Argyle ; and at Coupeville by Mr. Thomas Murphine.   Mr. W. H. Thacker made a reconnaissance on the San Juan Islands.   The Expedition is especially indebted to Mr. Alexander McDonald for permission to explore on his land in

---

[1] Native Races of the Pacific States, Vol. IV, p. 739.          [2] Ibid., pp. 737-739.

LOCATION OF CAIRNS,
SHELL-HEAPS, & TRENCHES.

MOUND .................................
CAIRNS (REPORTED)..........
CAIRNS (SEEN)....................
SHELL-HEAPS.......................
PETROGLYPHS.....................
TRENCH & EMBANKMENT........

SCALE OF MILES
0    10    20    30

North Saanich.   To Mr. Frederic T. Lazenby, who had explored burial-mounds near Port Hammond and Hatzic, we are indebted for the privilege of publishing his notes.   The accompanying diagrams and plates are from sketches and photographs by the respective explorers, and the illustrations of specimens are from drawings made by Mr. Rudolf Weber. ,

The accompanying map shows the locations of typical cairns, so far as known. These structures are usually situated on slopes with gravelly soil, and strewn with angular bowlders.   They overlook, or at least are near, the sea.   At many places the single cairns are about twenty feet apart.   Locations of shell-heaps and trenches are also given on this map.

The most northwesterly cairns known are on top of the bluff at Cape Lazo, about four miles northeast of Comox.   They are small, largely made up of gravel, and the skeletons found in them were almost entirely decomposed.   At the base of the bluff is a small shell-heap.

Small cairns of the usual type were found near Courtney, on the ridge back of the Indian potato-patches which are situated west of the shell-heap that extends along the southern branch of the Comox River.   Other mounds or cairns were situated near Courtney, on the slope south of the Mission Church and northern road.   These were composed of pebbles and fragments of rock from an inch to three inches in diameter, and of loam.   They resemble the natural mounds on the prairies south of Tacoma, Wash., and are probably of similar origin, as no artificial structure, artifacts, or bones were found in them.   There are several shell-heaps at the same place.   Cairns are said to have been found on the hillside that descends to the Indian village about a mile west of Comox in the direction of Courtney, between the northern and southern roads.   They were destroyed by the road-builders.

A cairn was found on Denman Island at the western end of a small shell-heap that extends along the northern end of the island, and two more cairns were seen at the base of the high bluff on the eastern side of the north point of the island. These cairns on Denman Island were of the usual type, but rather small.

Mr. Deans reports that at Nanoose, about twelve miles north of Nanaimo, there are " cairns of earth " in which Indians made intrusive burials.

At Port Hammond and Hatzic, B. C., were a few burial-mounds which in some respects resembled the cairns under discussion.

At Point Roberts, Wash., on the southern end of the shell-heap situated at the eastern end of the bluff, were a series of burials, which, although covered with bowlders, differed in many respects from typical cairns.

Cairns are found at several places on the islands of the San Juan Group, which lie directly across Haro Strait, east from Victoria.

Small cairns were found on every point of land on the bay at North Saanich, which is fifteen miles north of Victoria.

Mr. Argyle discovered others on a point at Sidney, about two miles south of North Saanich, and on a point about a mile northeast of North Saanich.   Mr.

Hastings reports them on Salt Spring Island, which is about five miles northward from North Saanich.

About four miles northeast of Victoria, on land belonging to the Hudson Bay Company, and sloping eastward towards Cadboro Bay, were several hundred cairns made of bowlders, apparently taken from a parent outcrop at this place. It was here that Messrs. Deans, Hastings, Newcombe, and other members of the Natural History Society of Victoria, as well as Professor Boas, Professor Von den Steinen, and Dr. Dorsey, made their principal examinations of cairns. Here and generally in the vicinity of Victoria the custom of constructing cairns seems to have had its highest development. The type of structure appears to have undergone modifications with increasing distance from this point.

Due east of this group, close to the beach on the south end of a little point, were a few small cairn-like structures. The north end of the point was cut off by a dry moat. Here were found traces of house sites, and two skeletons covered with a few stones.

Cairns also exist on Discovery Island, due east of Oak Bay, and not far from Victoria. Professor Boas observed many at Parsons Bridge, south of the Gorge. According to Mr. James Deans, there are cairns on the Hudson Bay Farm, east of the Victoria and Nanaimo Railroad and west of the Gorge. A druggist of Victoria reports cairns at Gordon Head, six miles from Victoria. Mr. Argyle reported some on Rocky Point, which is about twenty-two miles by road southwest of Victoria, in Metchosen County, and on Church Hill near Beecher Bay, a mile and a half beyond Rocky Point. Others are said to exist on the Pemberton Estate near McNeill Bay, and at Sooke, about six miles northwest of Beecher Bay.

On the south side of the Straits of San Juan de Fuca, cairns are reported at Port Angeles. On Whidbey Island, three miles and a half northwest from Coupeville, or a mile and a half west of San de Fuca, at the most westerly point of Penn Cove, were a number of small cairns made of angular bowlders. They were situated on the slopes near the beach, on both sides of a small ravine.

The cairns, so far as known, are always near shell-heaps; but the latter are so numerous all along the coast that their proximity does not necessarily imply an historical relation between the two kinds of structures. In the area of cairns human bones are rarely found in shell-heaps, except when a cairn has been erected over the latter. It seems, however, that a few skeletons found at Comox, North Saanich, and near Coupeville, are the remains of bodies buried on the shell-mound before it had reached its present height. It is only in the shell-mounds of Lower Fraser River that human remains are numerous. In the northern part of Vancouver Island and in Washington south of Coupeville, in which regions no cairns have been found, human remains seem to be absent from shell-heaps.

On the whole, the evidence furnished by the region from which we have the fullest data tends to show that at one time the cairns were the burial-places of the makers of the shell-heaps near by, but that on other occasions and in the same region people who made shell-heaps did not bury in cairns. The variation in form of the cairns seems to be due to the character of the material available for their construction and to the greater or less care taken, rather than to difference in plan. The various forms are more or less abundant wherever cairns are numerous. Those made of large bowlders are most common at Victoria, Coupeville, and other places where such materials occur. The most elaborate cairns, and the greatest variety, are found near Victoria.

Some cairns with an outer retaining-wall of stones and a cyst in the middle, such as have already been described, agree closely with the description of mounds given by Fowke.[1] In these latter, soil was used in place of small stones to fill in the spaces between the cyst and the retaining-wall. The transition from one form to the other is quite gradual. At Cadboro Bay both types are found at the same site (Plate IV). It would seem that some among the burial-mounds located along the Lower Fraser River, between Hatzic and Port Hammond,[2] may be considered as highly modified forms of cairns. No cairns made entirely of stone were found in the last-mentioned region.

Among the cairns at Cadboro Bay were a few rectangular enclosures, open on top, similar in form to the cysts in cairns. No remains were found in them (Plate V, Fig. 1). These may have been unused burial-places. There is no evidence that they were cairns opened by previous explorers. Such enclosures were all on high outcrops of rock near the centre of the burial-place.

The cairns were evidently all built on a well-defined plan, looking towards the construction of a central cyst, which, however, was often very poorly made.

In Nicola Valley in the interior of British Columbia (see " Memoirs Am. Mus. Nat. Hist.," Vol. II, pp. 405, 437, *et seq.*), in Montana, and in Idaho, graves are found in talus slopes. These graves are covered with piles of stone. None of them have cysts. Near the outlet of Nicola Lake and between Harrison Lake and Little Lillooet Lake, graves were found in which the body was buried in the ground. A few bowlders were placed on top of the grave. Both structures are entirely distinct from the cairns with central cyst which we are discussing here.

Near the head of Harrison Lake, at Point Roberts, in the shell-heaps of the Lower Fraser River, and in those near North Saanich and at Comox, graves were found which were covered by a few bowlders, like those just described ; but both skeletons and bowlders were covered by earth or shell-heap material.

At Point Roberts there were a number of pits, surrounded in some cases by bowlders. In one of these pits, covered by a few bowlders, several skeletons were found buried in one excavation, while cairns contain but one skeleton each. There were no objects with the skeletons found in these pits, which can hardly be classed with typical cairns.

---

[1] See p. 73 (Cairn 17) ; also Bancroft, Native Races of the Pacific States, Vol. IV, p. 737.

[2] Some of these were first explored in the summer of 1894 by Mr. Frederic T. Lazenby of Retford, Notts, England, during his residence in British Columbia (see p. 60).

The skulls from the cairns give evidence that the people practised the same methods of deforming the head that were in common use in this area until recent times.   A skull from Coupeville ($\frac{99}{2676}$) shows the characteristic deformation of the Chinook heads, in which forehead and occiput are so much flattened as to be nearly parallel.   Most of the skulls from Victoria and vicinity are flattened to a less extent.   A few skulls found near Victoria and at North Saanich suggest a method of deformation somewhat similar to that practised by the Kwakiutl, which consists of a combination of antero-posterior and lateral pressure, and results in a narrowing and lengthening of the skull.   On the whole, however, antero-posterior flattening seems to have been used most extensively.

### DETAILED ACCOUNTS OF EXPLORATIONS.

### PORT HAMMOND (by Harlan I. Smith).

A burial-mound made of earth was found about a mile north of the shell-heap bordering the north side of Fraser River at Port Hammond.   It was on the border of Pitt Meadows, measured twenty-four feet in diameter by five feet in height, was of the usual circular mound form, and below the surface layer was composed of yellow clay.   Extending through the mound, on a level with the surface of the surrounding forest, was a stratum of vegetable mould averaging half an inch in thickness.   Near the centre of the mound this stratum contained pieces of charcoal, burned clay, and ashes, barely sufficient to be the result of the cremation of a body.   Below this stratum was the natural surface soil, and about one foot lower down the yellow clay subsoil.

Another mound, situated on the bluff overlooking Fraser River, just above the shell-heap at Port Hammond, was explored by Mr. Lazenby in 1894. He reports that it was a simple mound of circular outline and about ten feet high, composed of a surface layer of vegetable mould, and under this of sandy soil similar to that found in the neighborhood.   There were no bowlders in it; a skeleton was found stretched out at full length on its back, in a good state of preservation, unaccompanied by objects; the skull was short; and the Indians knew nothing of the mound, and had no legend about it.   Only three cases have come to my notice in which ancient skeletons have been found stretched out at full length, although I have opened several hundred graves in British Columbia.

### HATZIC [1] (by Frederic T. Lazenby).

Circular mounds of earth similar to the one at Port Hammond were found at Hatzic on Fraser River, several of them having interior stone cysts and circular rows of small stones.   Three of these mounds were explored in the summer of 1894.   The Indians have no more knowledge of them than of the one at Port Hammond.

---

[1] A description of mounds at this place is given by Mr. Charles Hill-Tout on pp. 114–122 of his paper " Later Prehistoric Man in British Columbia," published in Vol. I, Sect. II, Trans. Roy. Soc. Canada, Second Series, 1895–96.

No. 1 stood on the edge of a depression which had formerly been a water-course in the bottom-land, subject to overflow, erosion, and deposition of the Fraser. In its reduced condition, it was about 24 ft. in diameter at the base, and almost flat on top over a space 14 ft. in diameter. It was 7 ft. high. On the top had been a cedar-tree which was about 8 ft. in diameter. Around the base of the mound, on a level with the surrounding surface, were large bowlders laid within an inch or two of each other. These formed a rude circle of single bowlders. No mound was found in which such stones formed squares, nor were they laid more than one tier high. Such stones are not found on the bottom-land at this place, and these may have been brought in canoes up the water-course from the shores of Hatzic Lake. They were probably originally outside of the mound, and were nearly covered by soil washed down from it. A second row of bowlders, similar in all respects to the first, was about 18 ft. in diameter. The cyst was about 4 ft. square, and 3 ft. high. It was covered with a flat stone, which fell in when the cyst was disturbed. Above it were traces of a fire and various strata, as is usual in mounds. The body had been buried in a flexed position, facing east. The skull was long, the hair rusty black. A copper needle 7 in. long, and $\frac{3}{8}$ in. thick at the base, which appeared to have been broken, and three oblong copper plates [1] $3\frac{1}{2}$ in. long by $2\frac{1}{4}$ in. wide and $\frac{1}{16}$ in. thick, with an oblong hole in the middle of each, were found in the cyst, enclosed in cedar-bark 3 in. thick. A small piece of woven fabric, made of the wool of the mountain-goat, was also found.

No. 2 is under part of the Canadian Pacific Railway embankment. Externally it presents the features of No. 1. It contains a cyst, which, being under the railroad, was not opened.

No. 3 was on the south side of the railroad, slightly to the west of No. 1. In the cyst was found the skull of a woman, but the other bones were disintegrated. The skull was long. A copper ring enclosed in cedar-bark, and a long strand of hair, were found with it.

## POINT ROBERTS (by Harlan I. Smith).

At Point Roberts pits from five feet to fifteen feet in diameter by from three to five feet deep were found. They contained human skeletons. In some cases, bowlders stood around the edge of the pit, and others covered the skeletons. Dr. R. Eden Walker of New Westminster, who described these pits to us, designated them as wells with paved bottoms which covered graves. Our excavations showed about two feet of vegetable mould in the bottom of the pits, which extended down into the shell-mound material. In one pit four skeletons were found. The bones were disarranged, showing that the position of the skeletons must have been changed after burial. Over them were traces of wood, and above these bowlders. The whole suggests that the bodies had been placed in boxes, and that these boxes were buried in pits and covered with bowlders. When the boxes decayed, the bowlders fell down into the pit. The skeletons ($\frac{99}{1907}$) were found at a depth of from two to three feet below the bottom of the pit. There were no objects with them.

## SAN JUAN GROUP (by W. H. Thacker[2]).

The skeletons found in the cairns of the San Juan Islands lay usually on the surface of the soil or in an excavation about a foot deep, over which bowlders were piled until an oblong cairn was formed, six to twelve feet long by from five

---

[1] According to the description by Mr. Lazenby, these copper objects resemble the specimen found in Cairn No. 17 at North Saanich (see Fig. 2 on p. 65), and the facts about the three mounds strongly suggest that they were simply cairns covered with earth.—H. I. S.

[2] Mr. Thacker first published some of these notes in The American Archæologist, Vol. II, Part 4 (April, 1898), p. 97.

to nine feet wide and from two to four feet high.    Some of the cairns are so old
that the stones have settled deep into the ground.    Especially was this the case
with some found on the most northerly point of San Juan Island.    These cairns
appeared the most ancient among those found.    Nearly all seemed to have had
earth scattered over them.    Ashes and charcoal were found over the skeletons,
all of which were charred.    The cairn stones, however, showed no signs of having

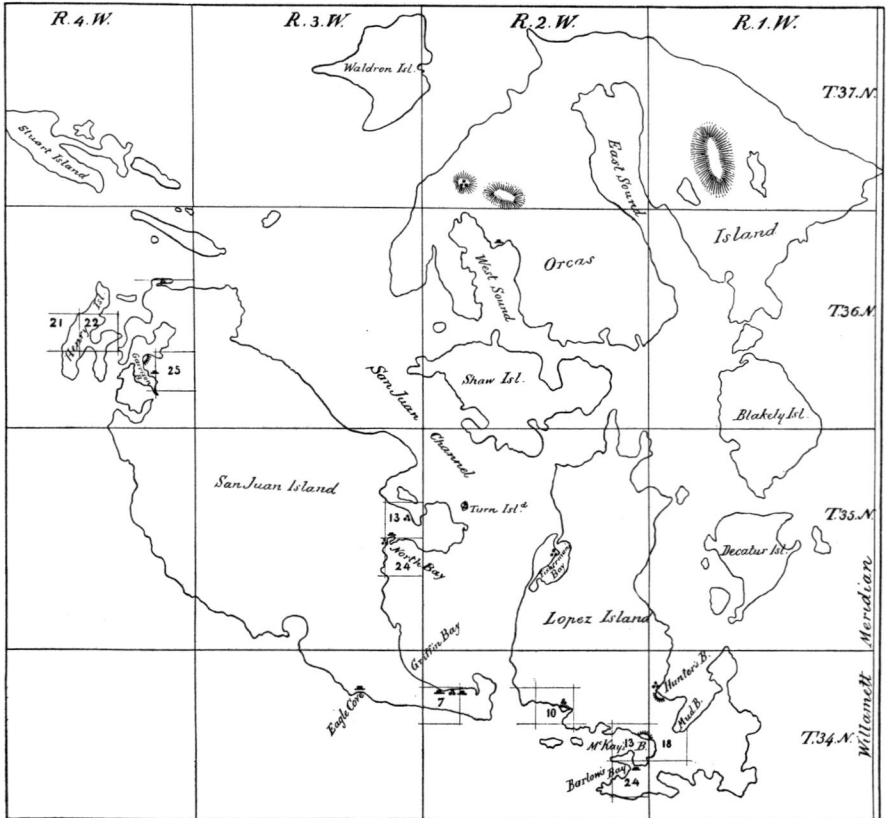

Fig. 1.   Map of San Juan Group, showing Location of Cairns.

been burned ; still it is possible that the bodies were cremated after being placed
in the cyst of the cairn.    With one exception, the skeletons were found flexed.
No objects were found with them, except a slate fish-knife, which was apparently
put in with material used in making the cairn.

In a number of mounds, most of which are situated on headlands, the skeleton was found surrounded by a wall of stones, generally placed on edge and

capped by a large bowlder.   The sides of these cysts were from four to six feet long.   Their height was about three feet.   The skeletons were much charred, and above them ashes and charcoal were found.   Following is a detailed description : —

No. 1.   Cairn located near a shell-heap and a spring on San Juan Island, at a point extending into North Bay (see Fig. 1).   It was the largest found on the San Juan Group, being 25 ft. square, 2 ft. high at the corners, and 5 ft. high in the centre.   The sides ran north and south, and east and west.   It was made up of large bowlders, the lower ones being placed on edge.   A trench extended around the cairn, from which was probably taken the earth which covered it.   The cyst was small, and contained a little ash only.

No. 2.   Cairn situated within a few yards of No. 1.   It was 12 ft. long, 8 ft. wide, and about 3 ft. high.   In the cyst a charred skeleton was found stretched out at full length.

Nos. 3 and 4.   Cairns located on a steep bluff 200 ft. high, north of North Bay.

Graves under stone-heaps were located between the shell-heaps on San Juan Island, on the south shore of Griffin Bay.

No. 5.   Grave located on the north side of an ancient trench, not far from a bluff on the southwest side of Lopez Island.   It was not covered with stones, and was oblong in outline.   A short distance to the north of this are a number of small stone cairns.

Cairns are also located on the shores of Hunter's Bay, Lopez Island.

No. 6.   Cairn on top of Bald Knob, or Orcas Knob, sometimes also known as "The Head of Turtle-Back Mountain."   This is on Orcas Island, some distance north of the north end of West Sound.   It was 10 ft. square and 3 ft. high.

No. 7.   Cairn located on Turn Island, on low land, within 30 ft. of the beach.   It was 7 ft. by 9 ft. in outline and 3 ft. high.   It was neatly formed, rounded up in the centre, and lightly covered with earth.   On top rested a bowlder weighing about 1000 pounds.

A number of cairns were located near Fisherman's Bay on Lopez Island.   One of these was 12 ft. long by 8 ft. wide and about 3 ft. high.   Over it some earth was heaped.   The body had been placed on the ground in a flexed position.   The skeleton was partly burned, fragments of the femora and vertebræ remaining.   Ashes and charcoal were found with it.   A fir-tree nearly 6 ft. in diameter stood near the cairn, and its roots extended through it, showing that the tree had grown up since the erection of the cairn.

## NORTH SAANICH (by Harlan I. Smith).

Many of the cairns at North Saanich were built on top of the shell-heap which is parallel to the beach at the post-office.   Some appeared like a small outcrop, but on excavation proved to be cairns with cysts, some of them five feet in length, made of bowlders weighing several hundred pounds.   The best-made of these cysts were somewhat rectangular, the straightest sides of the bowlders being placed inward.   They were covered with slab-shaped stones having at least one straight side, which was placed downward.   Usually the stones forming the cyst constituted the greater part of the structure.   The pile was made up of few and comparatively small stones.

There were also found cairns so rude that no cyst could be recognized.   They were simply stone piles, or a few heavy bowlders placed on top of the skeletons.   In some of these rude cairns there was a row of stones placed around the body and the material covering it.   In these the skeletons usually rested on the natural surface of the soil, the cairn being built over it.   In some cairns with regular cysts the skeletons were found four feet deep.   Several cairns were covered and filled with clay, so that they appeared like some of the mounds at Hatzic, but were much smaller (Plate III, Fig. 2).   On the whole, the cairns of this place are smaller than those found at Victoria.

In the cairns, well-preserved skeletons (Plate III, Fig. 1) were usually found, although some were charred, and a few were much decayed.   They were in a better state of preservation than any found by us near Victoria, but this does not necessarily indicate that the burials were more recent, since more favorable physical or chemical conditions of the soil would prevent rapid decomposition.   In 1898 we explored twenty-one cairns at this place, a detailed description of which follows.   Nos. 11–21 were on the north side of the bay.

### *Cairns explored in 1898.*

No. 1.   On point S. E. of post-office.   Its cyst was embedded in the shell-heap, and only a single stone protruded above the surface.   About 6 in. below the surface the other stones were found, forming a cyst 2 ft. deep, 3 ft. wide, and 5 ft. long.   The side stones were large, and reached to the bottom of the cairn.   The cover-stones were large, and flat on one side.   The fact that small barnacles still adhered to some of these stones proves that they were taken up from the beach.   A fir-tree one foot in diameter was growing up through the cairn.   Skeleton $(\frac{99}{1028})$ in burned soil mixed with shell, flexed, on right side, head N. E., face W., hands over head.   A chipped arrow-point $(\frac{146}{5137})$ was found in cyst.

No. 2.   5 yds. E. of No. 1.   A fir-tree 4 ft. in diameter, probably over two hundred years old, over cairn ; roots 8 in. thick over skeleton.   Cyst 16 in. deep in soil, 3 ft. wide, 5 ft. long, similar to that of No. 1.   Skeleton $(\frac{99}{1029})$ in loam mixed with shell, flexed, on left side, head S., face W.

No. 3.   75 yds. S. of No. 2.   Formed of a greater number of stones than either No. 1 or No. 2.   Cyst 2 ft. deep, 4 ft. wide, 6 ft. long.   Skeleton $(\frac{99}{1030})$ in loam mixed with shell, on right side, head N., face W.

No. 4.   About 25 yds. W. S. W. from No. 3.   Cyst 3 ft. deep, 4 ft. wide, 5 ft. long.   Only a single stone projected above the surface.   A large stone $(\frac{146}{5147})$ in which a small mortar had been made was used as a cover-stone over the skull.   Skeleton $(\frac{99}{1101})$ flexed, on right side, head N., face W.

No. 5.   About 17 yds. N. of No. 4.   The stones, 8 in number, showed partly above the surface of the soil, and seemed to be merely a retaining row on one side of the body.   Skeleton $(\frac{98}{1032})$ covered with 14 in. of soil, flexed, head N., face W.

No. 6.   40 yds. N. of No. 5.   Cyst similar to that of No. 1, 3 ft. deep, 4 ft. wide, 5 ft. long.   Some shells $(\frac{146}{5141})$ found in the cyst.   Head of skeleton $(\frac{99}{1103})$ W., face S.

No. 7.   10 yds. N. of No. 6.   Cyst 16 in. deep, 3 ft. wide, 4 ft. 6 in. long.   Skull and some bones badly burned, but the surrounding ground and the shells, which constituted part of the soil, showed no signs of fire.   Head of skeleton $(\frac{99}{1104})$ W.

No. 8.   About 40 yds. S. by W. of No. 7, on western slope of shell-mound.   Cyst well formed, 1 ft. 6 in. deep, 4 ft. wide, 5 ft. long.   Part of one of the cyst stones visible above the surface.   Head of skeleton $(\frac{99}{1105})$ S. E., face N.

No. 9.   100 yds. N. of No. 8, on western slope of shell-mound.   Cyst well formed, two of its stones projecting above the surface.   Skeleton $(\frac{99}{1033})$ on shell material $(\frac{146}{5130})$, unusually large ; leg-bones out of place, being separated from the pelvis.

No. 9½.   1 yd. N. of No. 9.   Skeleton burned.

No. 10.   About 13½ yds. N. of No. 9, on western slope of shell-mound.   A skull $(\frac{99}{1107})$ and part of a rib were found 2 in. below surface in shell material ($\frac{5168}{3}$) next to a bowlder. Probably this was not a cairn, but the bones, after rolling about, happened to find a resting-place under the shelter of the stone.

No. 11. On the point across the bay N. of post-office. There were a great number of stones visible on the surface, and the whole structure was larger than those on the south side. In form it was similar to No. 1. Cyst 1 ft. 6 in. deep, 4 ft. wide, 6 ft. long. Head of skeleton ($\frac{1888}{T}$) N. W., crushed.

No. 12. $6\frac{2}{3}$ yds. W. from No. 11, unusually large, about 8 or 9 ft. wide and 12 ft. long, sides and ends straight. Cyst well formed, 3 ft. deep, 4 ft. wide, 5 ft. long. Skull ($\frac{188}{T}$) crushed in soil ($\frac{5168}{3}$).

No. 13. $8\frac{1}{3}$ yds. W. of No. 11. Cyst well defined on surface, 1 ft. 4 in. deep, 1 ft. 6 in. wide, 3 ft. 6 in. long, similar to No. 1. Head of skeleton ($\frac{189}{T}$) S. W., face S.

No. 14. 15 yds. W. of No. 11. Cyst 2 ft. deep, 3 ft. wide, 4 ft. long, similar to No. 1. Skeleton ($\frac{199}{T}$) on right side, head W., face S. A slate knife ($\frac{5168}{3}$) and an elk-tooth ($\frac{5162}{3}$) were found here.

No. 15. 40 yds. N. W. of No. 11. The bowlders were 1 ft. below the surface, so that the cairn was hardly visible. Cyst 2 ft. 6 in. deep, 2 ft. wide, 4 ft. long. Head of skeleton ($\frac{192}{T}$) E.

No. 16. $33\frac{1}{3}$ yds. W. of No. 11. Cyst 3 ft. deep, 4 ft. wide, 4 ft. long, made of unusually large stones. Large roots of a fir-tree were growing through the skeleton. Head of skeleton ($\frac{193}{T}$) N. E.

No. 17. 150 yds. N. of No. 11, on the west slope of the shell-mound, about 15 yds. from the beach. It was rectangular in outline and unusually large : 9 ft. wide, 12 ft. long. One large stone in the N. W. end was higher than the rest, and protruded 18 in. above the surface of the soil. Cyst 4 ft. deep, 4 ft. wide, 6 ft. long, well made, with large thin cover-stones. Above, extending to the top of the projecting stones, and less than one foot below the surface, was a layer of soil. Skeleton ($\frac{194}{T}$) in centre of cyst, flexed, head N. W. A copper object (Fig. 2) with small hole near one side, evidently for suspension, was found at the head. It resembles in form the copper ornaments found in the Thompson River region (see Figs. 87–89 and Figs. 365–366, Vol. II), and appears to be in two layers. Perhaps we have here two specimens cemented together by copper salts. Part of a pestle and a stone ($\frac{5168}{3}$, $\frac{5161}{3}$) were also found in this grave, but they probably belonged to the shell-heap refuse into which the cyst extended.

Fig. 2 ($\frac{189}{T}$). Copper Ornament found in Cairn No. 17, North Saanich, B. C., 1898. (Greatest diameter, 45 mm.)

No. 18. About 50 yds. S. of No. 17, in the same shell-mound. It was barely under the surface, and was covered with stones. The skull of the skeleton found in this cairn was missing.

Nos. 19, 20, 21. On a point about half a mile N. E. of No. 11. Skeletons in cysts. In the first two of these all the bones were decomposed. The skeleton in No. 21 was charred.

## Cairns explored in 1899.

No. 1. On point N. W. of post-office, and about 40 yds. W. of No. 11 (explored in 1898). Poorly made. Cyst ill-defined, covered with bowlders weighing about 300 pounds. Skeleton ($\frac{2991}{2}$) 2 ft. deep in soil, flexed, face N.

No. 2. 5 yds. W. of No. 1. Composed mainly of two flat stones placed over the skeleton. Skeleton ($\frac{2992}{2}$) 3 in. deep in soil, flexed, on left side ; hands near neck, which was directed southward ; skull missing.

No. 3. A rude stone heap near No. 2. Skeleton ($\frac{2993}{2}$) 1 ft. deep in soil, flexed, on right side, head E., face down. Charcoal and ashes were found in the soil below the skeleton.

No. 4. About $6\frac{2}{3}$ yds. E. of No. 2, about 6 ft. wide by 9 ft. long. Cyst disturbed by scrub fir-tree 6 ft. 1 in. in circumference, which grew over it. Skeleton ($\frac{2994}{2}$) that of a child. The roots of the tree had pushed the skull about two feet from its natural place, and it was impossible to secure some of the bones. Originally the head had been directed towards the northwest.

No. 5.   On the next point N. E. of Nos. 1, 2, 3, and 4, about 4 ft. wide by 6 ft. long.   Skeleton ($\frac{88}{2835}$) 1 ft. 6 in. in clay subsoil, flexed, head N. E., face down.   The right femur is smaller than the left.

No. 6.   About 25 yds. N. E. of No. 4, about 2 ft. deep, 6 ft. wide, 10 ft. long.   Skeleton ($\frac{88}{2836}$) flexed, head N.

No. 7.   A pile of stones without cyst on northern end of Shell Island, a small island about two miles E. N. E. of post-office.   Skeleton ($\frac{88}{2837}$) only 4 in. deep in soil, flexed, head S. E., face down.

No. 8.   On the next island to the east, which is somewhat larger.   5 ft. wide by 9 ft. long. Skeleton ($\frac{88}{2838}$) on the surface, covered first with earth and then with bowlders, flexed, head N., and partly burned, although there was no evidence of fire in cairn.

No. 9.   On Shell Island.   Head of skeleton ($\frac{88}{2839}$) S. W.   All the bones were more or less burned, but no evidence of fire in the cairn was detected.

No. 10.   On point about a mile S. S. E. of post-office,[1] about 4 ft. wide by 8 ft. long.   Seven stones projected above the surface, one at the head end and another at the foot end being specially prominent.   No cyst.   Skeleton ($\frac{88}{2840}$) 10 in. deep in loam mixed with shell, flexed, head N. E.

No. 11.   Near No. 10.   Skeleton ($\frac{88}{2841}$) on surface of soil, flexed, head N. W.   The skull was the only part not burned.   It was covered by stones.

Nos. 12 and 13.   In close contact, forming one oblong mass of bowlders, extending from S. W. to N. E.   No. 12 formed of seven large stones enclosing skeleton.   Skeleton ($\frac{88}{2842}$) on surface of soil, covered with gravel and shell fragments showing surf-worn edges, flexed, on back, head S., hands crossed over the chest.   No. 13 formed of bowlders enclosing skeleton.   Some of them were taken from the beach.   Skeleton ($\frac{88}{2843}$) on surface of soil, covered with gravel and shell-heap material to a depth of 4 in., flexed, head S. E.

Nos. 14 and 15.   A short distance E. of Nos. 12 and 13, and also forming a group (see Plate III, Fig. 1);   No. 15 being N. N. W. of No. 14.   Some of the bowlders found in these cairns were from the beach.   Some were covered with barnacles, and others were rounded and smooth.   The stones surrounded the skeletons.   Skeleton in No. 14 ($\frac{88}{2844}$) on surface of soil, covered with gravel and surf-worn shell fragments mixed with charcoal, a large stone slab resting on top of this material ; flexed, on left side, head S. S. E., hands to face.   Skeleton in No. 15 ($\frac{88}{2845}$) on the right side, slightly flexed, head S. S. E., face N. E. ;   right arm extended along the side, and flexed to shoulder ; left upper arm extended along the side, and forearm crossed over the body.

No. 16.   10 yds. W. of No. 15, 4 ft. wide by 5 ft. long.   Three stones only projected above the surface ; but there were about sixty, weighing from 25 to 75 pounds each, in the cairn, below the surface of the soil, which was mixed with shells to a depth of about 6 inches.   Skeleton ($\frac{88}{2846}$) 2 ft. 6 in. deep in soil, flexed, head S.   The bones were much more decomposed than those in either No. 14 or No. 15.   A Douglas fir-tree 3 ft. in diameter stood on top of the cairn ; and the roots, one of which was over 8 in. in diameter, grew over the femurs, and had displaced the skeleton.

No. 17.   About 200 yds. W. of No. 16.   It was about 1 ft. 6 in. high, and filled to a level with the highest bowlders with yellow clay, which probably originally covered the cairn.   This feature is decidedly striking when compared to cairns like No. 14, in which the skeleton is found on the natural surface of the soil, surrounded by a row of bowlders, and covered with gravel.   Skeleton ($\frac{88}{2847}$) in cyst in centre of cairn, on clay subsoil 2 ft. 6 in. below top of cairn, or about 1 ft. below the natural surface ; flexed ; head W. N. W.   It was much decomposed.   Several barnacles and crabs were found with it.[2]

No. 18.   10 yds. W. N. W. of No. 17, and similar to it in appearance.   Skeleton ($\frac{88}{2848}$) 14 in. deep in mixture of clay and loam, flexed, head N. W., face S.   Several crabs were found with it.

No. 19 (Plate III, Fig. 2).   15 yds. S. W. of No. 18, 1 ft. 6 in. high, 4 ft. wide, 6 ft. long.

---

[1] Three additional cairns at this place contained skeletons that were almost completely cremated.

[2] Several cairns similar to this one, and near it, were not examined, as large trees, which we were not allowed to disturb, were growing over them.

Like No. 17, it was filled to the level of the highest bowlders with yellow clay, which probably originally covered the cairn. Skeleton ($\frac{299}{840}$) in a mixture of clay and earth at a depth of 3 ft. from surface, or 4 ft. 6 in. from top of cairn, flexed, head N. W., face E. A Douglas fir-tree about 3 ft. in diameter stood at the foot of the cairn ; and some of its roots, over 8 in. in diameter, extended over the skeleton.

No. 20 (Plate III, Fig. 2). 5 yds. N. W. of No. 19, and similar to it. A few clam-shells were in the grave. Skeleton ($\frac{299}{850}$), that of a child, 3 feet below surface, or 4 ft. 6 in. from top of cairn, flexed, head N. W., face S.

No. 21. 5 yds. S. S. W. of No. 20. 1 ft. 6 in. high, 8 ft. wide, 10 ft. long. Cyst 2 ft. wide by 3 ft. long, extending 1 ft. 6 in. down below the surface, or 3 ft. below top of cairn, made of large bowlders, with large flat cover-stones. Over the top of these was about 8 in. of earth ; and then to the top of the cairn were bowlders, between which was a mixture of clay and earth. Skeleton ($\frac{299}{851}$) 3 ft. below surface, or 4 ft. 6 in. below top of cairn, flexed, head N. N. W., face S. Three crabs and some shell-heap refuse and charcoal were found in the grave. Crabs were not found in cairns except in this immediate vicinity and on this particular point.

No. 22. 3 yds. S by E. of No. 21, 1 ft. high, 2 ft. wide, 3 ft. long. Some charcoal was found in the grave. Skeleton ($\frac{299}{852}$) 3 ft. below the surface or 4 ft. below top of cairn, flexed, head N. W., face S.

No. 23. 50 yds. S. W. of No. 22, 1 ft. high. An arbutus-tree 3 feet in diameter, and a fir of about the same size, were both growing to the S. E. of the cairn. Their roots extended over the skeleton Skeleton ($\frac{299}{853}$) 2 ft. 6 in. deep in soil, flexed, head S., face N. E.

No. 25. On the third point S. E. of post-office, 1 ft. 6 in. high, 6 ft. wide, 8 ft. long. Cyst poorly formed, being composed simply of a single row of stones, against which the skeleton lay. Skeleton ($\frac{299}{855}$) in shell-mound material, flexed, on the back, head N. W.

No. 26. 5 yds. N. W. of No. 25. Only a single stone covered the skeleton. Skeleton ($\frac{299}{856}$) 1 ft. deep in hard clay, flexed, head N. W.

No. 27. 100 yds. N. E. of No. 26, 1 ft. 6 in. deep, 3 ft. wide, 5 ft. long. Skeleton ($\frac{299}{857}$) flexed, head S., face down.

No 28. 20 yds N. of No. 27, 6 ft. long by 5 ft. wide. One of the cover-stones weighed about 500 pounds. Skeleton ($\frac{299}{858}$) in cyst, flexed, head N. W., face N. E.

No. 29. 15 yds. N. of No. 28, 3 ft. high, 6 ft. wide, 8 ft. long. Cyst covered by a bowlder weighing about 700 pounds. Some shell-heap material was in the grave. Skeleton ($\frac{299}{859}$) flexed, head N. ; roots of a fir-tree 3 feet in diameter extended over it.

No. 30. 20 yds. N. of No. 29 Skeleton ($\frac{299}{860}$) flexed, head N., face S. E. ; roots of a fir-tree 4 ft. in diameter extended over it.

## CADBORO BAY, NEAR VICTORIA, B. C.

Cairns are very numerous at this point. Many have been opened at different times by various parties. In October, 1897, twenty-one were explored by Harlan I. Smith ; while in April of the following year a like number were investigated by Gerard Fowke.

### Report of Harlan I. Smith.

No. 1. Approximately rectangular, 10 ft. S. E. and N. W. by 11 ft. N. E. and S. W. ; maximum height above surface of surrounding field, 16 in., grave extending down about 3 in. into the gravelly subsoil, and covered by two large stones. No traces of bones.

No. 2. A typical small cairn partly filled in with earth, 1 ft. 5 in. high, 9 ft. E. and W., 8 ft 6 in. N. and S. This cairn was not excavated by us.

No. 3. This appeared to be a simple conical pile of stones, without cyst or special cover-stones, 1 ft. high, 8 ft. in diameter. In the grave, which extended to the gravel below, there was no trace of bones.

No. 4. A typical example of the large stone heaps.

No. 5. In this cairn irregular bowlders projected above the other cairn stones. Two pieces of broken shell and a little charcoal were found in its cyst.

No. 6 (Fig. 3; Plate V, Fig. 1). This structure is a nearly square enclosure, made up of six large bowlders and some small stones resting upon an outcrop near the crest of the hill rising westward from Cadboro Bay. The straightest sides of the six large bowlders are turned inward, and so the walls of the cyst are fairly straight. The enclosure was clean, save for less than two inches of moss growing on the bed-rock, while rubble and bowlders were banked up on the outside of the cyst.

Nos. 7, 7a. Enclosures similar to the preceding, extending nearly E. and W., and a short distance S. W. of No. 6, No. 7a being the most southerly. Three circles, each about 3 ft. in diameter, and formed of small bowlders, were in contact with No. 7a, — one N., one S., and one at the S. W. corner. Four lines of small bowlders radiated from the same enclosure, — two westward, slightly diverging; one to the north; and one to the northeast. These circles and lines are very crude, being barely discernible, as the ground is so strewn with bowlders that lines and circles may be imagined in many directions. Cattle and sheep graze on these grounds, and disarrange bowlders of the size composing these structures. It is said that the latter have been kept in repair by the recent settlers. Their repairs probably account for the regularity of the circles and lines. The central stones of the cairns and enclosures are of such size that they could not be disarranged by cattle. Mr. Deans states that some years ago he saw Indians who said that they had seen such enclosures used in ceremonies, and that fires were built in them. A natural crack in the rock was pointed out by him as a blood-trough. With the exception of a few particles of decayed bone found in No. 7, no bone, ashes, or charcoal was found, other than might easily be accounted for by the log-fires made during the clearing of the land by the Hudson Bay Company.

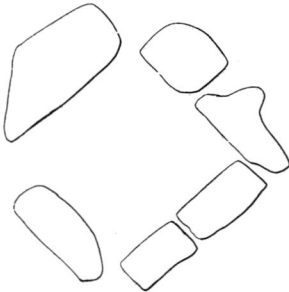

Fig. 3. Plan of Enclosure No. 6, Cadboro Bay, near Victoria, B. C., 1897. (Scale, 1 : 54.)

No. 8. A rather rude cairn 8 ft. in diameter E. and W. by 10 ft. N. and S., and 1 ft. 5 in. high. Among the top stones was found a granite object of ellipsoid shape, with a saucer-shaped depression at the ends of the short diameter (Fig. 4). It may have been artificially formed, and, if so, is the only stone object, to our knowledge, found among the bowlders of a cairn. It is much weathered. A portion of a skull was found in the cairn at the southern end of the grave, which was hollowed down into the yellow gravel below the layer of dark surface soil.

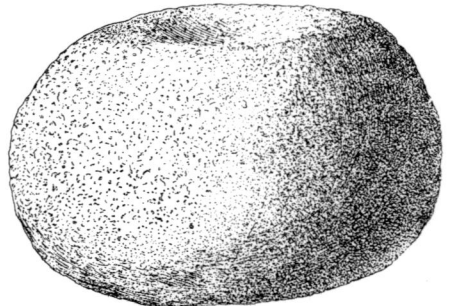

Fig. 4 (2⅓₀). Granite Object found on Cairn No. 8, Cadboro Bay, near Victoria, B. C., 1897. (Width, 144 mm.)

Nos. 9, 9a, 9b. Three cairns, the first two of which were respectively 15 ft. 10 in. and 16 ft. 6 in. in diameter, No. 9a being 20 ft. S. of No. 9. The third cairn (9b) was 18 ft. 6 in. E. of No. 9a, and had been opened. The relative distance between these cairns indicates their great frequency at this place.

Nos. 10, 10a (Plate V, Fig. 2). No. 10, a cairn 12 ft. in diameter, the top of the largest stone projecting 3 ft. above the ground.   This is an example of cairns in which a very large bowl-der was used to form one side of the cyst.   The structure was built up at one side of the large bowlder.   This cairn was not excavated by us.   No. 10a, a cairn 12 ft. E. of No. 10, 13 ft. in diam-eter, its highest stone extending 2 ft. 2 in. above the surface of the ground.   Its cyst was evenly walled, especially along the eastern side, by turning inward the smoothest and straightest sides of the bowlders used in its construction.   It was rectangular, and extended N. and S.   Not all cysts extend in this direction.   No trace of bones remained in it.

In one other cairn a disintegrated skull was found at the north end of the grave.   The legs were flexed.   The bones were much decayed, and resembled fine gray powder.   In all of the other cairns, except No. 8, the bones were entirely decayed.   Other cairns explored yielded no additional information.

## Report of Gerard Fowke.

A very few of the cairns explored were found to contain skeletons in a fairly complete state of preservation.   Occasionally it was possible to secure nearly every bone; in others the remains were in such condition that while small or thin bones crumbled on exposure to the air, larger and more solid ones could be removed if sufficient care were exercised.   In most, however, the frame was so decayed and soft as to preclude exhumation of any of its parts, while in some no trace of bone could be seen.   This difference in condition does not necessarily indicate that a great length of time intervened between early and later burials; it is due principally to the varying capacity of the soil for retaining moisture.

All excavators agree in the statement that with the exception of a small piece of copper, no artificially shaped objects of any character were discovered in the graves.   Except that no bones were found whose condition allowed of their removal unbroken, the results corresponded with those of previous explorers.

The first foot or thereabouts from the surface of the ground is composed of a very loose, dark, fertile loam; a hole made in this, filled again with the material that was taken out, presents no marks by which its limits may be determined. For this reason it sometimes happens that the margin of a cairn, the outline of a grave, or the depth of a burial-pit, is not to be ascertained with exactness.   Below the surface soil is a mixture of sand and gravel, packed quite hard, some of it due to disintegration of the native rock (a diorite or trap), but the greater part being a glacial deposit, granitic in character.   An excavation in this, refilled with the sub-stance removed, will, under ordinary circumstances, be always easily traceable; for the undisturbed deposit is usually more or less stratified, and when once loosened will not pack in as solid as it was at first.   When the yellow sand and the dark superficial earth are intermingled, as is the case in most of these graves, the line of demarkation between the untouched earth and that which has been re-placed is distinct.   No special effort was made to form a symmetrical or sharp-ly defined grave.   Indeed, with rude tools accuracy would be difficult or even impossible of achievement.   In every case it was plain that the hole had been scooped out in the beginning to a size sufficient for its intended purpose, without particular care or thought as to what the exact dimensions might be; and when completed, large stones were rolled on in such a manner as to cover and protect it. Consequently measurements given in the following report are only approximate, for under such conditions precision is unattainable.

The breadth of a cairn is measured across its centre, between the outermost stones which appear to retain their original positions; the height is from the general plane of the present surface to the tops of the highest stones. The diameter of a grave is measured at the top of the sand and gravel underlying the dark soil; its depth is the vertical distance from the plane of the general level to the lowest undisturbed earth. As a rule, the grave-pit extends about ten inches into the hard-packed subsoil, though sometimes as little as eight or as much as fourteen inches, depending somewhat upon the nature of the underlying material. The outline sketches show plans of the cairns as they would appear if all the stones were smoothly planed off at the surface of the ground. To avoid confusion, only such are shown as belong to the grave proper, those of the protective tumulus being omitted. Following is a detailed report of my explorations of twenty-one cairns.

No. 1. A cairn of circular outline (Fig. 5), consisting of a row of eleven bowlders from a foot to two feet in diameter, enclosing a space 5 ft. by 5 ft. 6 in. across, longest from N. E. to S. W. The area within was filled to a height of 18 in. with stones from an ounce to fifty pounds in weight; the larger ones were at the bottom, and extended well below the surface. A few inches of earth separated them from fragments of a skull, crushed flat, on undisturbed sand, at a depth of 30 in.

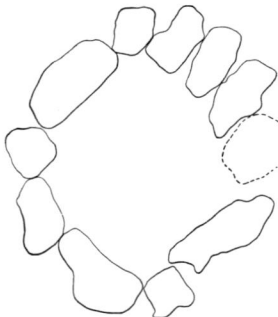

Fig. 5. Plan of Grave-stones in Cairn No. 1, Cadboro Bay, near Victoria, B. C., 1898. (Scale, 1 : 54.)

No. 2. A grave, the west side of which was formed of a large bowlder, in place, with one flat surface nearly vertical and lying N. and S. The east side and the ends were formed by six bowlders, weighing from 200 to 500 pounds each (Plate II, Fig. 1). The space surrounded by them measured 6 ft. N. and S. by 2 ft. 6 in. E. and W. Besides many smaller stones, there were within this area four bowlders of from 150 to 250 pounds each; a few inches of earth separated the latter from a fragmentary skeleton at a depth of 2 ft. The body had been flexed, but not closely, and laid in on the side with the head north. The bottom of the grave was a flat rock of gneiss or schist, in its natural position, and extending beyond the excavation on every side.

Fig. 6. Plan of Wall and Covering-stones in Cairn No. 3, Cadboro Bay, near Victoria, B. C., 1898. (Scale, 1 : 54.)

No. 3. A rudely rectangular cairn, measuring 14 ft. N. to S., 9 ft. 6 in. E. to W., and 2 ft. 6 in. high. After a wagon-load of stones of various sizes, up to 75 pounds, had been thrown aside, twelve very large bowlders and five smaller ones were found, so arranged as to surround a space 6 ft. by 9 ft., the sides practically parallel with those of the cairn. The interior was nearly filled by three bowlders measuring respectively in their three dimensions 30 × 22 × 15 in., 34 × 28 × 18 in., and 40 × 26 × 16 in. (Fig. 6). All were laid with the longest diameter across the grave and the shortest axis vertical. The earth was undisturbed in the southern half of the enclosure. The central covering-stone lay partly over a circular grave-pit 36 in. in diameter, which extended well under the northern stone. This was filled with loosely-packed fine earth, and its bottom was 18 in. beneath the overlying bowlder. Close to the southern margin was a skull artificially flattened and laterally compressed.

No. 4. A small cairn, being only 7 ft. in diameter and a few inches high. A mass of small cobble-stones and pebbles was piled over six stones of 100 pounds weight or more, which covered a grave 3 ft. 6 in. in diameter and 2 ft. 7 in. in depth. At the bottom of this was a closely flexed skeleton, laid on right side, head W. The skull was flattened from glabella to vertex and from crown to base.

No. 5. A cairn covering a space 8 ft. 9 in. by 7 ft. 8 in., being longest N. E. and S. W. A bowlder 45 × 23 × 22 in. lay in the western half of the cairn, its top almost level with the surrounding surface. Under its centre was a skull, flattened front and back ; the remainder of the skeleton, which was flexed and placed on its right side, lay toward the middle of the cairn. A layer of fine yellow sand extended over the body. Two other bowlders, much smaller than the first, completed the covering of the grave, which was 3 ft. deep and the same in diameter. The cairn itself consisted of a single thickness or layer of small stones, covering and surrounding these bowlders.

No. 6. A circular cairn 14 ft. in diameter and 3 ft. high. Points of very large rocks projected from its top, the spaces between them being filled with smaller stones of varying sizes, from bowlders a foot in thickness down to fine gravel. When these were cleared away, eight large bowlders appeared. One of them, the highest, was in its natural place ; an excavation by the side of this, and extending partially under it, had been carried to a depth of 20 in., and contained a grave-pit 28 in. across. Nothing was found in it except a single fragment of a parietal bone. It was impossible to tell in what position the body had been interred. The grave had been nearly filled with earth, and the other seven bowlders rolled next to the one in place. The eight covered an area of 9 ft. by 10 ft. 6 in., longest N. and S.

No. 7 was rudely square in form, with each side 11 ft. long. On the southern side, stones were placed close together in two parallel rows a foot apart, extending to a distance of 8 ft. at a right angle from the edge of the cairn. On the north side two similar rows 3 ft. apart reached out 4 ft., and were connected at the ends by other stones. The earth under and about these rows had no appearance of any previous disturbance. All the stones, including those of the cairn itself, were small, none weighing over 50 pounds. Under the centre of the cairn was a grave 2 ft. 6 in. in diameter and 1 ft. 6 in. deep. No trace of bones remained in it.

No. 8. A cairn measuring 10 ft. by 12 ft., longest N. and S. Two large angular bowlders, in place, formed an end and a side of the grave, and six others in a rude arc completed an enclosure within which lay three covering bowlders. All except the two in place were rounded by weathering and ice-action, and weighed from 200 to 400 pounds each. The grave was somewhat elliptical, extending 3 ft. 6 in. N. W. and S. E. by 2 ft. 9 in. across ; it was more shallow than usual, being but 1 ft. 4 in. in depth. Only small fragments of bones were found ; sufficient, however, to show that the head lay toward the south.

No. 9. A practically square cairn, measuring 15 ft. across and 2 ft. 6 in. high (Fig. 7). The corners were approximately toward the cardinal points. A row of stones surrounded the base ; some of these weighed from 150 to 250 pounds. Inside of this rectangle was another 7 ft. 5 in. by 5 ft. 9 in. in extent, being longest from S. E. to N. W. It was outlined by stones from 40 to 60 pounds in weight laid on the original surface. The intervening space was filled with earth, pebbles, and cobble-stones. The inner row surrounded five large stones ; underneath these, a foot below the general level of the ground, was still another rectangle of cobble-stones and small angular fragments enclosing a space 2 ft. 4 in. by 3 ft. 4 in. (Plate II, Fig. 2). This bordered the margin of a grave whose bottom was 8 in. below the level at which they rested.   In it was a flexed skeleton, on the left side, head S. E.   The skull was somewhat flattened on the forehead, but was normal in other

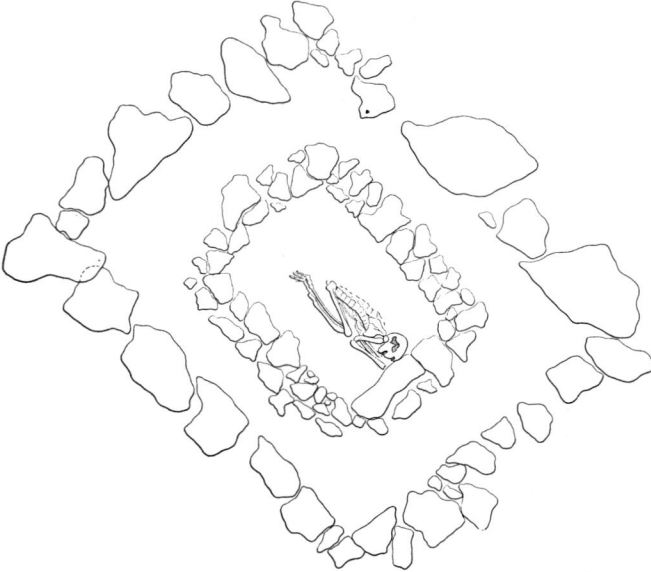

respects.   Some of the teeth were much worn.

No. 10.   A rectangular cairn 12 ft. 6 in. N. and S., 10 ft. 6 in. E. and W., and 2 ft. 9 in. high. The upper portion was composed of small stones. When they were removed, there was left an irregular wall or row of stones surrounding ten large covering-bowlders (Fig. 8); of these, five were sub-angular or fragmental, and five somewhat flattened or slab-like.   One of the latter, at the north end, and four of the former, were laid flat; the others were inclined at various angles.   Some of them extended into the earth fully a foot lower than the surface level.   The deepest were separated by

Fig. 17.   Plan of the Two Inner Rectangles and Position of Skeleton in Cairn No. 9, Cadboro Bay, near Victoria, B. C., 1898.   (Scale, 1 : 36.)

five or six inches of earth from a rectangular grave-pit 2 ft. 8 in. by 3 ft. 4 in., longest N. and S. It contained a closely flexed skeleton, laid on left side, head S.   The forehead was flattened. but otherwise the skull was of ordinary shape. Some small angular stones lay scattered along the margin of the pit, but not in contact except near the head.

No. 11.   A cairn, two sides of which, the north and the east, each formed a nearly straight line, and the rest of the perimeter an irregular curve.   It extended 15 ft. N. and S., 11 ft. 6 in. E. and W., and was 3 ft. high (Plate IV, Fig. 1).   The outer margin was of rather large rocks firmly embedded in the earth ; within, on the surface, were many covering-rocks of varying sizes, fifteen of which were so large as to tax two men with hand-spikes to the limit of their strength in removing them.   Some were in such position as to form a rude half-circle between 8 ft. and 9 ft. across ; this arrangement may have been accidental.   A rectangular grave, 2 ft. 6 in. by 3 ft., longest N. and S., had a depth of 2 ft.

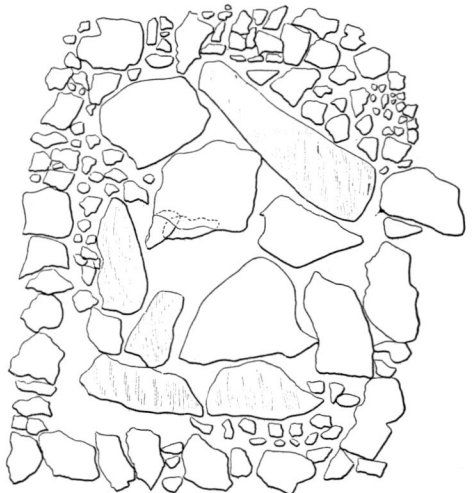

Fig. 8.   Plan of Wall and Covering-stones in Cairn No. 10, Cadboro Bay, near Victoria, B. C., 1898.   (Scale, 1 : 54.   Shaded stones stood on edge.)

9 in. The north end and about half of each side adjacent had a few cobble-stones placed within the margin of the grave-pit. Traces of bone were found, but not enough to determine the position of the skeleton. The bottom of the grave was quite muddy.

No. 12. A cairn with a circular outline 11 ft. in diameter and a height of 3 ft. It was covered with cobble-stones and small pebbles. When these were cleared away, four large bowlders were disclosed. One, measuring 30 × 36 × 30 in., was placed at the centre of the cairn ; the other three, flat or slab-like, were leaning against it on the west, north, and east sides, at angles of from 45 to 75 degrees. A smaller one, on edge, was between those to the north and east. Around these covering-stones a row of rounded bowlders formed an irregular circle 9 ft. N. and S. by 8 ft. E. and W. Under the central stone were traces of a flexed skeleton, on right side, head N. Nothing was left of it except the fragmentary skull, which was rather thick and heavy, and somewhat flattened at the front and back. The body had been covered and surrounded with small stones, and the large bowlder at the centre rolled directly on these. The grave was between 2 ft. 6 in. and 3 ft. in diameter and a little less than 2 ft. 6 in. deep.

No. 13. A cairn that had been somewhat lowered and altered in shape by hauling stones away from it ; but the base and margin were intact. The outline formed a regular rectangle 16 ft. by 20 ft., longest from N. to S. It was probably never much higher than when explored, — about 2 ft. 6 in., — though it may have had a more symmetrical outline. Only pebbles, cobble-stones, and small angular fragments were left ; all larger stones had been removed. The grave was under the flat central stone and the stone next north of it. It was 3 ft. 4 in. long, 2 ft. 9 in. across, and roughly elliptical in outline. Around one-half of the grave — that portion under the central stone — was a row of angular rocks from 5 to 25 pounds in weight. No trace of bone remained ; but there was evidence of decayed wood, which may, however, have been only the residue of a large root introduced by natural means.

No. 14. A cairn composed mainly of eight large and four small bowlders enclosing a rectangular space 6 ft. 6 in. by 8 ft., longest E. and W. The top was uniform in level with the general surface, giving the structure an unfinished appearance. On clearing off the top, an angular flat stone was found at the centre, surrounded by eight bowlders weighing from twenty to sixty pounds each. Under the central stone, with but an inch or two of earth intervening, lay traces of a skeleton. Only small fragments of bone were to be seen ; enough, however, to show that the head had lain toward the south.

No. 15. A cairn measuring 10 ft. from E. to W., 7 ft. 6 in. N. and S., and 1 ft. 8 in. in height. It was surrounded by ten bowlders from a foot to three feet in diameter, placed at irregular intervals. There were eleven large stones in the central part, lying in or extending a little below the natural soil. Below these were loose, dark earth, in a roughly rectangular space of 40 in. by 50 in. No trace of bone was left. The bottom, of compact gravel, was level and comparatively dry, and from 6 in. to 12 in. below the covering-stones.

No. 16. A cairn with four nearly straight sides, running nearly due N.–S. and E.–W. It was 10 ft. in length, 8 ft. in width at the east end, 7 ft. at the west end, and 1 ft. 6 in. high. In it was a grave 4 ft. 3 in. E. and W., 2 ft. 8 in. N. and S., and 2 ft. 9 in. in depth. On the bottom was a skeleton, flexed, on left side, head W. Four rocks covered the cavity, and rested directly on the bones, which were very soft and crushed into fragments. One of the covering-rocks lay on the skull and pressed it forcibly against a large stone, in place, which formed the west end of the grave. The fragments of skull were in such condition that its shape could not be ascertained.

No. 17 (Plate IV, Fig. 2). In external appearance, an earth mound, standing on the gentle slope of a still-water sand and gravel deposit. It measured 18 ft. in diameter and 3 ft. high, with a slight depression 4 ft. wide around it, from which earth had been taken to cover the cairn. This depression is nowhere more than 6 in. deep at present, but was much deeper when made. There were ten or twelve cubic yards of earth, with which were mingled a few small bowlders, covering a cairn made of six large and ten smaller stones (Fig. 9) ; the larger weighed from 200 to 500 pounds each, the smaller from 20 to 75 pounds. They covered an area 6 ft. 6 in. by 8 ft., nearly rectangular in outline, longest E. and W.   Under these stones were six others from 20 to 50 pounds in weight ; and beneath the last, with from five to eight inches of earth intervening, were traces of a skeleton, flexed, on left side, head S.   The skull was so decayed and crushed that its original shape could not be determined ; the bone was quite thin, and three teeth found were much worn.   The grave containing these remains was 3 ft. 11 in. in diameter and 2 ft. 6 in. deep.

Fig. 9.   Plan of Stones in Cairn No. 17, Cadboro Bay, near Victoria, B. C., 1898.   (Scale, 1 : 54.)

No. 18.   A cairn partly covered with earth (Plate I, Fig. 1).   The tumulus had a rectangular outline measuring 10 ft. by 13 ft., with the longer axis N. and S.   It stood on a gentle slope, with a slight depression all round except at the south end. The earth was piled to a height of 2 ft. over a cairn composed of three main bowlders, each weighing about half a ton.   These surrounded and covered a grave nearly circular in outline, 3 ft. in diameter and 2 ft. in depth.   On the bottom of this, under nearly a foot of earth, lay a flexed skeleton, on left side, head S.   The skull, which was directly under the largest rock, was small, and flattened front and back.

No. 19.   An earth-covered cairn, standing on the brink of a terrace.   It was 12 ft. in diameter and 1 ft. 6 in. high, with a depression all round.   Being overgrown with grass, it was not sufficiently distinct to show in a photograph.   When the superincumbent earth was removed, the cairn was found to consist of three bowlders weighing from 300 to 800 pounds.   Beneath them, at a depth of 2 ft. 2 in., was a flexed skeleton, lying on the right side, head N.   The skull was crushed flat.   The skeleton was that of a young person, the second dentition not being completed.

No. 20.   A cairn, like the last three, covered with earth.   A shallow depression extended entirely round it.   The mound stood on the brink of a terrace, and was 12 ft. long from E. to W., 10 ft. in breadth, and 1 ft. 8 in. high.   Many stones showed above the sod, five of them projecting from 6 in. to 12 in. above its top.   One of these, in place, at the centre of the mound, was too large to move without mechanical aid ; it formed the western side of a grave-pit, the eastern edge of which was almost under the corresponding margin of the mound.   In the grave, at a depth of 2 ft. 10 in. below natural surface level, was a skeleton, flexed, on left side, back straight, head W.   The skull was crushed to small fragments.

No. 21.   A cairn consisting of a mass of granite and a number of bowlders (Plate I, Fig. 2). The granite, deeply embedded on a gentle eastern slope, and with a flat, vertical face on the lower side measuring 7 ft. 3 in. in length, formed the upper or western side of a grave which was covered with bowlders of various sizes.   In the bottom of the grave were a few fragments of human bones ; enough to show that the head had lain against the large rock, and the flexed skeleton towards the east.   The grave was shallow, and barely large enough to hold the body.

No. 22.   A cairn opened in 1897 by Mr. O. C. Hastings.   It had a well-defined wall on each side, built up of large bowlders.   The body, flexed, lay crosswise between these walls, in a grave surrounded with small stones.   The skeleton was entire and well preserved.

## WHIDBEY ISLAND (by Harlan I. Smith).

### Cairns explored in July, 1899.

The cairns on Whidbey Island resemble those found near Victoria more than do those of other places.   Many of them are built at the sides of large bowlders.   The body usually rests on the right side, with the head west and the face toward the largest bowlder, the small stones being at the back.

No. 1. A cairn 5 ft. in diameter, consisting of one very large bowlder, against which small stones were piled. The large bowlder was in front of the body, and formed the western side of the cyst. Each end consisted of one stone; and a wall made of several small stones formed the eastern side. Skeleton ($\frac{99}{2643}$) at a depth of 1 ft., flexed, on right side, head N., face W.

No. 2. A cairn similar to No. 1 in that it was built against a large bowlder, which formed the south side of the cyst. The body faced the large bowlder, while the opposite side was built of small stones, each end of a medium-sized bowlder. Skeleton ($\frac{99}{2644}$) at a depth of 2 ft., flexed, on right side, head W., face S., hands near the knees.

No. 3. A cairn formed of small bowlders irregularly placed. Skeleton ($\frac{99}{2645}$) at a depth of 2 ft., on face and chest, head S., and lower legs flexed over thighs; arms straight along sides of trunk, hands to the pelvis.

No. 4. A cairn similar to Nos. 1 and 2, in that the largest cyst bowlder was opposite the chest of the skeleton. This side of the cyst was pieced out at the foot by another bowlder. The foot and head of the cyst were each made of a single bowlder; while the northern side, being at the back of the skeleton, was formed of small stones. Skeleton ($\frac{99}{2646}$) at a depth of 2 ft. 6 in., flexed, on right side, head W.; upper arms extended out from the body, one hand being at the chin, the other to the knees.

No. 5. A rectangular cairn formed of small bowlders. It was not higher than the surrounding soil, but the bowlders extended down to the skeleton. Skeleton ($\frac{99}{2647}$) at a depth of 2 ft. 6 in., flexed, on right side, head S. W., hands over face.

No. 6. A cairn consisting of two large stones at the head and one at the foot, with many small bowlders over the skeleton. Skeleton ($\frac{99}{2648}$) at a depth of 3 ft., badly decomposed, head S. S. W.

No. 7. A cairn formed of a large bowlder in front of the skeleton, with a small one at the foot, another at the head, and small bowlders at the back. Skeleton ($\frac{99}{2649}$) at a depth of 2 ft., badly decomposed, flexed, on right side, head N. W.

No. 8. A cairn consisting of two large stones in front, one at the back, a small bowlder at the head, and another at the foot. Skeleton ($\frac{99}{2650}$) at a depth of 2 ft. 6 in., flexed, on right side, head W., hands to the hips.

No. 9. A cairn consisting of bowlders of medium size. Skeleton at a depth of 3 ft., much decomposed, flexed, on right side, head W., hands at the knees.

No. 10. A cairn consisting of one very large bowlder in front, projecting over a number of small stones. Skeleton ($\frac{99}{2651}$) at a depth of 3 ft., slightly flexed, on right side, head W., hands to face.

PLATE I.

# EXPLANATION OF PLATE I.

Fig. 1. — Cairn No. 18, Cadboro Bay, Victoria, B. C. (1898), partly covered with earth (see p. 74).
Fig. 2. — Cairn No. 21, Cadboro Bay, Victoria, B. C. (1898), composed of a mass of granite and a number of bowlders (see p. 74).

Fig. 1.

Fig. 2.

Cairns of British Columbia and Washington.

PLATE II.

# EXPLANATION OF PLATE II.

FIG. 1. — Cyst in Cairn No. 2, Cadboro Bay, near Victoria, B. C. (see p. 70).

FIG. 2. — Cyst in Cairn No. 9, Cadboro Bay, near Victoria B. C. (1898), composed of cobble-stones and small angular fragments (see p. 71).

FIG. 1.

FIG. 2.

Cairns of British Columbia and Washington.

PLATE III.

# EXPLANATION OF PLATE III.

Fig. 1. — Cairns Nos. 14 and 15, North Saanich, B. C. (1899), on the right and left respectively, opened, and showing skeletons (see p. 66).

Fig. 2. — Cairns Nos. 19 and 20, North Saanich, B. C., in right background and left foreground respectively, both filled with clay (see pp. 66, 67).

Fig. 1.

Fig. 2.

Cairns of British Columbia and Washington.

PLATE IV.

# EXPLANATION OF PLATE IV.

Fig. 1. — Cairn No. 11, Cadboro Bay, near Victoria, B. C. (1898), the outer margin formed of rather large rocks firmly embedded in earth, the top covered with numerous stones, the whole resembling a truncated pyramid (see p. 72).

Fig. 2. — Cairn No. 17, Cadboro Bay, near Victoria, B. C. (1898), in external appearance an earth mound, with slight depression 4 ft. wide around it, from which earth had been taken to cover the cairn (see p. 73).

Fig. 1.

Fig. 2.

Cairns of British Columbia and Washington.

PLATE V.

# EXPLANATION OF PLATE V.

FIG. 1. — Enclosure No. 6, Cadboro Bay, near Victoria, B. C. (1897), formed of six large bowlders and some small stones (see p. 68).

FIG. 2. — Cairns Nos. 10 and 10a, Cadboro Bay, near Victoria, B.C. (see pp. 68, 69).

Fig. 1.

Fig. 2.

Cairns of British Columbia and Washington.